Lessons from Stanley the Cat

THE SECOND EDITION
New color drawings and additional lessons
Nine Lives of Everyday Wisdom

Jennifer Freed Ph.D.

Illustrations by Tone Gellerstedt

Copyright © 2016 Dr. Jennifer Freed

All rights reserved under Copyright Conventions. No portion of this book may be reproduced in any form, electronic or otherwise, for any purpose, without the prior written permission of the author.

Published by Mermaids Press
Santa Barbara, California

To my mother, Nancy Lee, who taught me to deeply love the beyond-human world

INTRODUCTION TO THE SECOND EDITION

We are thrilled to present our second edition of LESSONS FROM STANLEY THE CAT.
In this edition you will find original color drawings by our Swedish Artist Tone Gellerstedt, and some new original pages. We hope that you will continue to enjoy Stanley for many years and pass his lessons on to everyone you know. Stanley keeps his presence known in my life through vivid dreams, and reminds me to live with joy and gratitude.

Table of Contents

Introduction 1
1 – You and Yourself 6
2 - You and Others 21
3 - Love and Lust 44
4 - Healthy Habits 58
Stay Connected to Stanley 86
Acknowledgments 87

Introduction

For thirty years, it's been my job to study and understand the vicissitudes of human strengths and weaknesses. I've consulted on thousands of psychotherapy cases in my career; I've written books about character, compassion, sexuality, and personality. Everything I learn, I pass on, so that people may live more gracefully in the worlds they inhabit. And, who, people have asked, has been by my side inspiring me through all these years as a seasoned psychotherapist and educator?

My cat, Stanley.

Stanley was the love of my life. This is something I try not to say too often because my mate gets offended and gives me the dagger eye. Stanley and I were together for almost twenty years, and he continues to be my greatest teacher, as I believe his lessons are timeless. Some people may say I am twisted for giving a cat such status and respect, but one thing years of practicing and teaching psychotherapy have taught me: you cannot judge a *living master* by his cover, and humans often overrate their importance on planet Earth.

When you come across an enlightened being it is best to drop judgments and receive the lessons. Stanley, through his remarkable life and his evolved death, shared his wisdom with all creatures he encountered.

To help him reach the greatest possible audience, Stanley and I became a teaching team. He demonstrated and I witnessed. He showed me the way, and I faithfully translated his wisdom into human signs and symbols. His paw prints have marked my soul indelibly. Stanley is the teacher; I the devoted scribe.

When Stanley first moved in with me as a small kitten, we cuddled endlessly, entwined as one. He preferred affection, at any time, to food. Sometimes when I left the house early I was seized by the thought of him alone in the house. When I would come through the door at night, he was never shy to run to me, to listen to every detail of my day, to follow me around the kitchen as I prepared a meal. In short, Stanley and I lived in a mobile and indestructible bubble of bliss.

Our first test was when he became dangerously ill with bronchitis. I stayed up with him three nights in a row as he wheezed like a chain saw in my face. He never complained; he simply huddled as close as he could to me and gasped for air as his nose clogged with what seemed like superglue. Three days of sleepless nursing tested our bond, yet even that became a proof of some type of selfless love, a love that could endure all.

When he was well, I nuzzled his downy face and he would nuzzle mine in return. He learned early on how to come up and press his purring softness into my face. He was especially gifted at knowing just when to do that when I was crying or upset.

To say that Stanley was a wild man would be an understatement. He was fearlessly drawn to the outdoors and would coax me at all hours to break routine and join the cacophony, or silence, of the wildlife just outside our downtown cottage.

One of his habits was to wander in and out of the bedroom during the night. We slept with the bedroom door open to the backyard. We felt safe enough, and living in Santa Barbara afforded us consistently benign weather. At first I was so attuned to his every movement that I would awaken each time he sauntered out under the moonlight. But as time wore on he became like a mist drifting in and out, and when his warm supple body quietly pushed up against mine, I would feel a sense of grace, and primordial comfort.

During our first two years together, I was studying madly as I was a newly appointed chair of a program in psychology. I learned soon that even books were offensive to Stanley's aesthetic. He would be so bold as to swat at the book I was reading with contempt, or place some part of his body between the page and me. I became more and more preoccupied with my work and studies, and this is when Stanley found the comforts of food. He had always maintained a firm physique when we were first together, even though his gait was more languorous than athletic. However now his shape was following his sybaritic appetite, and he was growing round. Some of my dearest friends would be rude enough to comment. I could tell it hurt him, but he always maintained his indifference to public opinion and would wear his size with an almost Roman pride.

When Stanley was about five years old, I was called away for work for a month long training program. Whenever I would call home, I was told that Stanley was nowhere to be found. I started imagining the worst. He didn't say goodbye and he wasn't coming back.

When I finally returned home, it seemed as if the whole place had been holding its breath. That night I dreamed that I went everywhere just shouting Stanley's name. I felt as if the world had been suctioned dry of color. My heart hung like a broken and twisted branch. I went for days trying to catch a scent of him, harnessing my thoughts into a funnel of telepathic begging. "Please, Stanley, come home."

Then one morning, Stanley ambled into the bedroom. He casually lumbered in, looking around the room as if he had left something there, and sidled up to me. I covered him with kisses and tears. I tore at him with a joy and hatred so combined that I felt I had become the wild one. He just allowed me to grab at him. He said nothing and received my emotional pawing. He was back.

He was mine and we would never discuss it.

Months later, I met Rendy, the love of my life. It started innocently enough. We swam together. We worked together. Sometimes we would even dance together. Stanley started sensing that something was up and would stand in front of Rendy like a sentry. Then he would stare and walk past. He would never stoop to acting jealous.

Stanley watched our budding romance in his way: acceptance with distance. He did occasionally push Rendy's hand away from me or plant himself firmly where Rendy would want to sit or lay down. Soon, though, he was sleeping on the couch and resigning himself to bigger meals. We all fell into a rhythm of living together and sharing our affections.

This is when I began to see that Stanley had always been steering me toward my destiny with Rendy. He would not and could not offer me more than his devoted feline love. He even seemed happy at times to see me with someone who could make me giggle, who would read next to me and like it; someone who would talk to me on the phone for hours.

He was just there all along showing me what unconditional love looked like without any rules or expectations, and we both knew that, as a mere woman, I could not love the same way. I would always be mired by the more weakly human traits such as fear, insecurity, and jealousy and propelled by the peculiarly human ambitions, desires, and idealizations.

Stanley maintained his noble and unconstrained loving nature throughout his almost twenty years with me, and when it was his time to die he simply walked off into the woods near our home and left me his lifetime of wisdom and love.

The following pages are an invitation into a wry and loving look about what is best in our humanity, what helps us be the best we can be. Laugh, sigh, cry, and even grumble and then pass the lessons on to everyone you know ... The legend of Stanley wills this to be so!

1 – You and Yourself

Wake up each morning with a song in your heart. Sing out when you first see someone you know.

It is common to start the day with a little resistance and reluctance. Sleeping and dreaming are not easy things to leap up from. But if you wake with a catchy tune and a dream for the day, it makes a great beginning for whatever your day has in store for you.

Pursue your goals like prey. Take time to make a good plan and have the patience to follow through a number of times. Failure is simply another opportunity to create a different strategy. Do not take mistakes personally.

Successful creatures stay focused on their goals despite obstacles and setbacks. They know deep down that frustration can be the fuel for determination. When something does not go your way, it is a sign that you need to be more flexible in your approach and reset your expectations.

Confidence does not come from things going easily; it comes from facing adversity and rising to the challenge. You can and will succeed if you are willing to consider every failed attempt as an opportunity to learn more, regroup, and renew your commitment.

Do not let any bad comments or derision bother you. Consider negativity as passing gas.

Nothing is really as personal as it seems. Everyone's opinion vanishes eventually, so there is no point to recording it in your memory unless it truly inspires you. When someone says something unpleasant about you, imagine it wafting by like a foul odor, or a plume of smoke from a soot-filled fireplace.

It is much more important to build on your strengths and work hard to improve on your weaknesses than it is to entertain a destructive comment. People who spread negative words usually live in a fearful and unhappy world inside their own minds.

Genuine greatness is not measured by quantity. Encourage yourself to want less and do more with what you have.

Accumulating stuff is a habit of those who are more interested in having than giving. Having more than you really need is not a statement of happiness but a condition of trying to fill up the ennui with insatiable consumption. It is okay to play with pretty and shiny toys and to chase them down with faster and faster vehicles, yet the more stuff you have the more time you need to spend managing the stuff.

Wouldn't it feel great to help someone who has hardly anything have a little joy in their day? A truly wealthy soul is filled with gratitude and overflowing with generosity.

Do not get attached to any one place in your house. Explore all areas as potential recreational respites.

Humans are often too preoccupied with labels and fixed ideas. Don't take *living room*, *bedroom*, and *bathroom* so literally. You can live in a bathroom, you can sleep in a living room, and you can take baths outside in the rain.

Start reimagining that every space in your domicile is a potential spot for all sorts of activities. You can play hide-and-seek in any space, and you can chase mice in and out of any room. Have a meal in the bathroom. Trim your nails in the bedroom.

Take a nap in the kitchen. Re-create, don't stagnate.

Walk proud in the body you have and all will find you appealing.

If you walk in your body like you are a king or queen, then you will be seen that way. Size or age is not a determinant of sexy. Sexy is a state of mind.

Whether you are wearing sweatpants or a fancy designer piece, you emanate your sense of style by the way you hold yourself and present yourself to others. Wear your body like a crown for your spirit and you will feel deserving of the praise you receive.

Keep yourself well groomed and smelling wonderful. Everything will respond to you better.

Every day is an opportunity to look your best. That doesn't mean you will necessarily feel like making the effort. Even if you are staying on the couch and shedding hair over everything, groom as if the most important visitor of your life was about to walk through the door. You will like your own company better if you treat yourself like you matter, no matter what.

When in an unfamiliar situation, tune up your ears, eyes, and nose.

You will feel more confident and project more assuredness if you look and act alert in foreign situations. You may want to fold your arms and look down when you are nervous, but that tells others that you are easy prey.

Walk upright; keep your eyes scanning in a relaxed and steady way, and listen as if you had ears and eyes on all sides of your head. The more you can take in about your new environment, the more you can sense who and what is safe, and who and what may be threatening. The more faculties you keep awake and ready, the more adept you will be at handling anything, pleasant or unpleasant, that comes your way.

Trust your instincts and stay away from people or creatures who smell like bad things or who are in bad moods.

If you pay close attention, you will find that you can sense when someone is not going to be kind to you. They give off a certain odor of irritation and their posture looks cranky. There is no point in trying to smooth out someone else's foul mood. Keep your attitude clean and positive and eventually their dark cloud will pass.

Eliminate the rats in your life. You will feel less stressed.

There is no point trying to teach treacherous rats how to behave. Their beady eyes and twitching snouts tell you that they are up to no good. Rats always look sneaky and can't really look you in the eye because they are busy hiding things or deceiving you.

You will always try to second-guess rats because they disguise their true motives. Unless you have an acquired taste for nasty drama, rid your environments of rats. You will notice that it is much easier to put your feet up and not worry about who is scurrying down below.

You will never feel left out if you treasure your own company the most.

We often believe the grass is greener somewhere else, which it probably is, if you think about it. But if you are absorbed in the possibilities of the present, you really don't have time to be mind roaming in places you are not.

Within you, and all around you, is a universe of imagination, physical matter, and creative possibility. When alone, explore the vast frontiers of perception and experience, and don't waste a precious moment wishing you were somewhere else.

When you feel rejected and eat a little more than usual, give yourself a break. We all need comfort.

If you nibble on more than you had intended to, you may be tempted to just go on eating till you are stuffed. Instead of doing that, take a warm bath or read some uplifting poetry or prose, and appreciate your rounded tummy with a little pat. Climb some stairs or leap from chair to chair if you want to lighten the load.

When you stare into the void, allow yourself to become immersed without consideration. You will find it relaxing after a while.

Emptiness is not a problem unless it is in the food bowl. Whether you call it meditation, staring, or prayer, taking a period of time to do nothing is a miraculous antidote for stress and busyness. At first the mind will be restless as it is used to being assigned a thousand jobs at once. But if you keep with the practice of emptying the mind, after a while the thoughts are not as scattered and racy.

Do not let fame affect you in any way. You are never anyone other than who you really are.

People can get really hung up on what others think of them and who they imagine, or wish, themselves to be. The problem with this is that public opinion is an unstable pendulum and the most fickle indicator of popularity.

No matter how important you think you are, your self-importance never protects you against ill opinion, an ill body, or eventually death. A king of the forest is still just ordinary compost at the end. It is better to not inflate yourself with adoring fans and pumped-up self-images, because you are not made of anything fundamentally different than anyone else.

2 - You and Others

When you want to wake up someone you love in the morning, put your face gently to theirs.

Some of us wake up with a lot of vigor and drive. Others wake up like lazy dogs who would prefer to have the day start at noon. When you first approach someone who is struggling to open their eyes, it is wise to go in silently and smoothly for a soft face rub. When they feel you are a tender and fragrant companion, they can feel happy to open their eyes and see their waking dream sitting right next to them.

When you bring a gift to someone you love, place it in a special place where they are sure to see your effort and thoughtfulness. Look at them when they discover it and act joyful that they have received your gift.

Even if the recipient looks a little shocked, or scared at your choice of gift, they will be thankful that you care enough to go to the trouble to give something you hoped they would like. We all secretly wish for unexpected gifts. That is when we know someone is thinking of us, outside the realm of obligation.

Appreciate the people who feed you, provide you shelter, and work for you. Show them how grateful you are with consistent acts of affection.

You can often forget to acknowledge the simple gifts you receive daily. You can get used to what is given and forget that each small act of service is an act of love.

Imagine if everyone who does any small task for you on a regular basis were to stop abruptly. You can see that your life would be much harder in some important way. It takes such little effort, yet makes such a glorious impact, for us to show the helpers in our life some tangible appreciation for their generosity.

Do not let age, gender, race, economic, or species differences matter. In the eyes of Love, we are all here for the same reasons—to evolve, to learn, and to be close.

When your eyes are closed and you are near enough to someone, you can hear their heartbeat. The amazing thing is that everyone's heart is pretty much the same. Some of us move faster or slower than others, or to a different beat, yet what is on the inside is much more important, and longer lasting, than what is showing on the outside.

Nuzzle someone's head when their mind is overactive. Remind them to open up their mind to love.

The human brain is filled with frenetic thinking. The mind itself is a maze of memory, feeling, worrying, and planning. When the head is nuzzled, it harks back to a time when instinct was stronger than analysis.

Touching the head can evoke a warm and calming feeling. When the brain can let go a little of its millions of brainy missions, the body can open more and receive genuine contact. Rubbing or nuzzling the head can be the gateway to a new phase of contentment.

When someone is on the computer too long, help them by distracting them, or walk lightly on their keyboard.

This is perhaps one of the biggest challenges of living in a computer-driven nation. How do you get your beloved off the darn device? If a little nudging on the arm or a little repetitive pleading doesn't work, then a warning screech or a walk across the keyboard is fair game.

How did the machine become the be-all and end-all of human attention? Devices are wonderful helpers; however, they can never replace the grandeur of body touch and the splendor of screen less contact.

A good friend remembers you, and makes time to sit with you without judging or bragging.

Many connections may be useful and good to have, but a friend who likes your company without an agenda is certainly a precious gift. When someone visits you because they miss the sound of your voice, or the way you walk across the room, or even the way you slurp down your water, then you know they have really come to see *you*.

Just think how happy it makes someone when you remember to reach out to them just because you love them, not because you have anything important to ask or share. Everyone wants to be remembered for their naturally wonderful qualities that hardly anyone remembers to mention.

A good friend consistently tells you how gorgeous and wonderful you are, even when you may not be able to return the compliment.

Compliments or praise are ideally given when you are not fishing for a lovely tidbit in return. The hardest compliments to give are those that acknowledge a quality or talent that you do not have. Generosity of the heart is the most valuable asset you can have. It will never become depleted if you keep using this often underused and regenerative quality.

Do not be intimidated by bigger people or creatures. Be amused by them, and let them know that your curiosity is more powerful than their size.

People who carry big sticks and stomp loudly are usually trying to cover up for some major sense of inadequacy. You are not your physical size; you are the size of your character. When you are around people or creatures that make a huge point of demonstrating their physical proportions or material largesse, simply be entertained by their exaggerated performance.

If you can enjoy their inflated self-importance, they will probably relax because you are accepting them and making them feel secure. Then you might also get a word in edgewise.

Nothing is personal unless you take it that way. What people do and say reflects them perfectly.

People often yammer to themselves about what the mirror of life is reflecting to them. If you hear them like a cat does, you will just notice their gestures and facial expressions. You will see that most people don't have a very wide range of expressions because they take themselves wherever they go and repeat their patterned responses in any given situation.

So next time someone goes off on you, remember that this is their personal repertoire of responses and it would exist with or without you. If they have something useful for you to consider, listen closely. Otherwise, it is best to watch their show with detached interest. You can learn much about someone by the judgments they espouse.

When people are arguing, remove yourself politely from their company.

There is no point in listening to loud arguments. Verbal sparring that goes on ceaselessly rarely has a logical outcome. It is simply the case of two subjects not really listening to each other and getting overwrought because one hasn't convinced the other of their deeply fixed position. It is best to make a quiet exit from these battles and wait till the arguers have expended all their frustration before you seek their company.

You will always be appreciated if you do not add to an aggravation or try to solve a ridiculous spat. Act as if arguments are overrated.

Sometimes you need to take a firm stand to know how your values matter.

Even if you like to "go with the flow" most of the time, there will come times when you need to stand up for someone or something that needs your help.

It can be difficult to step out of your comfort zone and can even seem emotionally daring, but it would be a great disservice to your integrity to hold back when something matters deeply to you. People and other creatures are defined as much by what they don't do as what they do. It is worse to regret *not* acting on a cherished principle than to do what you know is right in the moment and suffer other's disapproval.

We are all woundable, no matter how big our defense or shield. This is important to remember when you feel like hurting someone.

Invincibility is for superheroes and even they have an Achilles' heel—no one stays on top of the totem pole forever.

The nicest creature can become a tyrant when they are mad and there is someone weaker to pick on. There can be a temporary feeling of satisfaction when you make someone feel as bad as you feel or inferior to you, but that feeling is short lasting. It usually builds an unrelenting hunger for more because the brain learns to crave those little rushes of adrenaline.

Empathy, on the other hand, is the antidote to power abuse. To develop empathy one must take time to feel what it is like to be vulnerable, to feel what it is like to be a baby, a cat, a poor person, a hungry person, a crippled person, or someone who seems completely unlike you.

If you spend all your time identifying with someone others who are just like you, or those more powerful than you, you are more likely to act out your aggression on someone who is different or weaker than you.

You can give up sleep when you need to soothe someone you love.

People lose a lot of precious sleep time by partying, watching TV, listening to talk radio, and reading late into the night. Every now and then a creature you love might be genuinely having a hard time during the night. They might be scared because they are about to go into surgery. They might be sad because they have lost someone they love. They might be upset because someone has harmed them.

If you love someone, it is important to sacrifice a little comfort for them. Lie next to them, or walk around with them as they fitfully go to every room looking for a place to rest, and help them quietly get through their sleepless night.

Sit quietly next to someone crying and look up at them compassionately. There is not really anything you have to say if you show them love.

Most people think they need to fix things or take the pain away when people cry. Humans were specifically designed to cry as a way of releasing pain and getting back to the softness of their hearts.

All you need to do is believe that they are helping themselves by freeing the pain. If you are present and open to their hurt, then they will be encouraged to shed their sorrow. If you are patient, you will see that they can get through it. Their face will actually look younger if they release that pent-up agony.

Be kind to the aged and the dying. They do not have many advocates or visitors, and it takes so little to let them know you are really their friend.

It seems the hardest thing for humans to remember is that everyone will die one day. Most people are trying to chase after their youth instead of cherishing the stages of life. Older beings need more care and often get less thoughtfulness from others. If everyone else weren't so busy trying to live it up, perhaps there would be more time to hang out with the slower among us. The aged may not be as fun and as sparkly as new toys and adventures, but the light and gratitude in their wizened eyes is worth the effort.

Be patient and affectionate with the young. They are usually reckless and uncoordinated emotionally, and you can show them how to be accepting and mature.

Adults are quite serious about being busy. Sometimes they are so busy making things work that they forget young ones need their attention. The young only become wise when adults invest in their character. You can send young ones to school. You can send them to camps. You can send them a lot of places. But you cannot send them the quality of your loving attention unless you are with them.

Forgive easily when someone hurts you accidentally, or even intentionally. The next moment is not the past.

Moods, opinions, and attachments can lead to rash behavior. Sometimes we do things without even knowing why, and then strongly regret them. Forgive all creatures, if you can. It hurts you more to hold on to resentments; grudges cause stress in your body.

When someone is touching you in the wrong way, a little scratch or bite will tell them to stop.

Only the slightest response is needed to tell them they have missed the sweet spot. If they do not respond to that signal, then make your needs known.

Most people are surprised by, yet quickly understand, the meaning of a swift and assertive rebuff. What pleasures you is up to you to define, to describe verbally, and to demonstrate physically.

If someone leaves you for a long trip, do not act eagerly upon their return. Wait till they shower you with incessant promises of love.

They need time to settle in and you need time to check them out and see if they still smell the same. You may need to get a full sense of how their trip affected them.

Act friendly, but a little distant, so they know you have been away, too. You have been up to all kinds of things that they do not know about either. You might have discovered all manners of games around the house and new places for nooky. Once they see how self-possessed you are, and how perfectly well you did without them, they may try to win back your affections in the most surprising and sumptuous ways.

When the object of your most intense affection is not available, do not dwell on this. Find other friends and interests that bring out the best in you.

All of us sometimes get stuck obsessively thinking about our one special other. We are most attractive when we have many loved ones and outlets for sharing. Spread your needs for attention and affection to a wider circle so no one person feels too pressured.

When someone you love comes home, it is best to be waiting outside for them; however, look as if you were busy doing something else.

Have you ever noticed the glee you feel when you see your beloved pull into the driveway? It is as if someone is delivering a present just for you.

Busy yourself straightening up the welcome mat, pruning flowers, or coming up front from the backyard. If you just happen to be there when they open the car door, you may catch that first look that attracted you in the first place. By looking busy—and gorgeous—you might strike her heart in just the right place and improve the chances of a lovely night at home.

3 - Love and Lust

When you do not feel beautiful, do not look in the mirror. Look into the eyes of people or creatures that love you. Everything else is temporary and matters very little.

When you look at yourself through the eyes of the appreciative other, it becomes easier to see your shining strengths and the beauty inside you. Your gorgeous essence can never be truly revealed without the dimension of relationship and the look in the eyes of someone who truly "gets you." Animated expression is always in response to something precious in the world seeing us. Everything comes more alive when it is pictured through the lens of love, and feline-colored glasses can really add something, too.

If your partner is not in the mood for intense contact, back off. Instead, give them ample affection and see if they need any help grooming or feeling more desirable.

You can't convince someone to get aroused or guilt them into wanting you. If someone is not in the mood for what you are offering, see what they are in the mood for.

Perhaps they want a meal made for them. Perhaps they want things to be cleaner. Perhaps they need a good cry, or they want to lay their head on your soft belly. Maybe they would like you to stroke their head or give them a bath. When you offer someone what they really want, there is an awfully good chance they will be more open to offering you what you would like later on.

Be faithful to those you love and show them how to love themselves daily—no matter what!

Everyone has a hard time liking themselves some days. You can stare in the mirror for a long time with a big worried frown on your face. You can walk around in our pajamas without bathing for a long time. You can even sit on a couch and eat bowls of the same thing, like cereal or ice cream, over and over.

When you see someone you love acting like this, remind them how much they are loved. Humans can easily forget that they are loveable. You can just set a quiet, confident, and humble example when this happens. Take extra care in grooming yourself and give them a loving nudge to play with you. Run around the house a few dozen times and do special antics that help them laugh, and not take this temporary state of self-pity too seriously.

When you feel possessive about someone who is giving attention to someone else, try to get in the middle of them and show both of them how much you love them.

When you feel jealous of someone you love giving attention to someone else, it is best to love both of them more. If you see that you are not the only object of love then celebrate the opportunity to see what is lovable about others.

If others around you are feeling especially amorous, allow yourself to feel the romantic contagion of their good feelings. Bask in the glow of love, wherever you experience it.

Sometimes it is tempting to feel sorry for ourselves if we are not with someone we love. We can feel envious of others who are expressing affection. You can decide instead to get a contact high from getting in on the wonderful atmosphere of people in love.

People in love are actually releasing positive pheromones and hormones. If you lean into the loving scene, you may benefit from these extra goodies.

Be creative sexually. Do not hesitate to find any location that pleases your animal appetite, as long as you are sensitive to those around you.

Beds are great for sleeping and often good for lovemaking, too. But let's face it, when the only place you do it is in the bed, it can lead to "bed death."

Experimentation is the key ingredient to maintain sexual interest. Something as wild and sacred as sex does not do well with routines. It would be like caging a lion and feeding it at the same time with the same thing each day. Don't kill the majesty of the primal force with laziness and predictability. Take your sexual play for a creative and safe spin.

Enjoy your sexuality regardless of the response you receive. It is your life force and it is gorgeous.

It is not up to others to validate your attractiveness. You were born with this terrific life force that is your own magic wand of red, libidinal energy. The secret of consistent and joyful sexuality is to claim your inherent talent to delight and enjoy yourself. You may then choose to share that deliciousness with chosen others.

When you want someone you love to touch you in a special place, nudge their hand right to the sweet spot.

Others don't always know what makes you happy. You are also changing all the time. You can help someone out by showing them what really makes your whiskers stand up. Encourage them by approvingly placing their hand where you would like it to be. Reward them with reciprocal gestures and loving hums or purrs.

Don't imagine that people remember what touch you like, either. It is okay to remind them again and again. Sometimes it even helps to come up with some choice moves that suggest touching you in certain places. Lying on your back with your head cutely tilted can jog their memory to pat your belly. Pushing your head into the palm of their hand can produce a good head rub and so on...

Never use force to get what you want. Make your play, but if it is not genuinely received then let it go.

Force is for pushing open stuck doors. Force is for turning over a can for food. Force is for pushing a little toy up the stairs.

Force is never for gaining affection or receiving touch. When force is applied to creatures you love, you will lose their respect and perhaps even their love. One can only invite others to play, and *no* has to be an acceptable answer. *Yes* feels so great when it is freely given because you know that you are wanted and that the desire is mutual.

Seduction is just the practice of artful stretching.

Work your body and your body will work for you! Keep your body lithe and lean and ready to dance. The body is your instrument and how you move it in front of others will send a message. If you carry your body like a heavy mood with serious and stiff tones, then you will attract pretty somber attention. If you express your body with gestures of rapture and grace, then you will attract refined and sophisticated admirers.

The more artfully you can stretch your limbs, and the more facially expressive you are, the more vivid and bright attention you will receive. To seduce is to cull someone's interest. What is more fascinating than someone who is light, playful, and joyfully expressive in their body?

Foreplay is *for play*. The best part of arousal is the chase. Don't get overly concerned with outcomes when you can truly enjoy the petting, the pursuing, the finding, the leaps, the rolls, and all the ways you can release your passionate joy.

Don't go so fast! People seem to want to get sex over with instead of relishing the buildup of luscious tension. Why make an amazing adventure three minutes when it could be thirty? Speed is great for running, and sometimes chasing, but speeding through sex can be a real disappointment.

Racing to that erotic finish line will usually cheat you and your partner of juicy contact and intimacy. If you actually become interested in all the ways you can tease each other for extended play, you will not only maximize the pleasure but also strengthen the bonds of connection.

Make pleasant sounds when you are being touched just how you like it.

Little pleasant murmurs and nods let a person know that they are on the right track of creating touch pleasure, and everyone wants to be competent at touching.

If you can steer them in the right direction and indicate the best level of intensity, then you will feel much more satisfied, and they will feel more confident to keep pleasing you. Don't let guessing games get in the way of mutual pleasure.

When you become satiated with affection, kindly withdraw and luxuriate in the glow of fullness.

When you are lucky enough to get the affection you desire so strongly, make the exit from that encounter as exquisite as the buildup to it.

Let the object of your affections see how much their love has meant to you by showing how full you feel and how grateful you are. Don't roll over or start mindlessly scratching yourself. Preen for them as if their love has made you king or queen for the day.

4 - Healthy Habits

You never have to wait for anyone, or anything, if you learn to find pleasure in the moment at hand.

Have you ever gotten really peeved because someone was late? That may never bother you again if you are completely present to the amazing world in front of you. Come to every event or moment as if it could be your last and you will see that there is always plenty of stimulation right then and there.

When you stop to reflect, make sure you are situated in just the right light.

You never know who is going to observe you when you take that special moment to daydream or be with your innermost thoughts.

If you manage to perch yourself in the best possible hues of natural or indoor light when you take a little silent time, you can be a powerful inspiration to someone who just happens to see you. It is like the "halo effect," when people stop in their tracks to gaze upon another as if they were an angel. This is a wonderful way to bring people spontaneously into sacred space.

Do not get so caught up in words and thoughts that you forget about nature.

People love to talk and think. Sometimes they forget that there is an entire world out there beyond talking and thinking. Nature has its own way of communicating through vibrant sounds and colors and nature doesn't demand analysis or chatting. In nature you can let your body experience the wild and uncivilized grace of a place without explanation.

It is important to return to the best side of your animal nature on occasion. When you nurture this "natural" part of you, you can actually gain internal peace from which you can take in more sensual pleasure and joy from your everyday life.

When in nature, look around silently and patiently, and you will marvel at the magnificence of even the simplest setting.

Even if you walk around your block ten times you can notice much more by being quiet and allowing the world to enter all your senses. Anyone can spend an hour just watching ants build their anthill and learn a tremendous amount about cooperation.

Too often we are looking for the big bang instead of the tiny game. The smallest attention to color in the landscape, temperature, sound, and texture will bring ecstasy to the panorama of your imagination.

Do not listen to music too loudly. Find a decibel level that is conducive to enjoyment, not overwhelm.

Human ears were made to hear very soft and far away noises for our survival. Crushing your eardrums with loud thumping beats is simply spitting at the work of art that is your incredibly sophisticated ear.

Ears are soft, fleshy, and highly advanced systems for refined listening. Treat your ears like the fine antennae that they are and you will hear many more birdsongs.

Never let people know how fast you are. Appear slow in all things, and less is expected of you.

Although you may pride yourself on how fast you can get things done, or how fast you can move, it can be a real curse if you let too many people know. Unless you want to stand out for your speed in life, then you'd better keep your productivity a well-kept secret. If you run fast when someone calls out your name, for example, then they may think that you will always come running. Act more casual about your competencies and people will not get overly ambitious and exploitive with your talents.

Never race toward anything unless you feel like getting some exercise.

All too often people are rushing toward their coffee, gulping down their food, hurrying through sex, and typing maniacally on their computers. Then they are often upset because they "never have enough time."

Time is not something that you have more of when you are speeding everywhere. It just makes life dizzily fast. If you actually breathe in each moment and focus on being relaxed wherever you are, time spent is infinitely more enjoyable and satisfying.

Trimming nails can make you seem friendlier.

Your nails are important to keep in tip-top shape. When they are caked with dirt, too long, or soiled with food, they are ghastly and unappealing, and possibly even threatening. When they are trimmed and cared for, people think you have overall good grooming habits.

Since most of us don't have good scratching posts at our disposal, consider carrying around a good nail file and clipper. You never know when you might have a little spare time to upgrade your appearance or let others know you that are not out to scratch them.

Meditation and yoga are helpful. Even if you cannot do most positions, or stay perfectly still, your presence is what matters.

Quieting the mind and keeping the body flexible are the keys to a healthy life. Even if you are restless and stiff you can gain a lot by making the effort to stretch and be peaceful. Life is not a competition regardless of how many rats you observe racing each other.

If you show up to yoga and meditation to be more mindful and harmonious, no matter how distracted and conflicted you feel, the rest of you will catch on eventually, or just catch the good vibes of others.

Jumping daily improves circulation and flexibility.

When you are young, you can't help but jump around. As you get older, it seems like there is less to jump up about. But if you practice leaping for joy, you may actually feel happier about things.

A little bounce in your step as you walk around the house, go to work, or even just get up from bed can perk up your heartbeat and your attitude.

Landing on your feet is the best option when trying leaps beyond your reach.

Always know where your feet are in any given situation. No matter how heady things may get, it is a good policy to keep your feet where you can find them. If you let any wild idea get the best of you and forget that everything that goes up must come down, you may crash headfirst. Ouch!

On the other hand, approach your biggest dreams with an understanding that you may take a fall. If you do plummet, you will have anticipated the velocity and distance better. Anyone can take a flying leap, but it takes someone with real panache to make a smooth landing or recover gracefully from a wipeout.

Take time out of your day to take time out of your day.

Sit quietly. Do nothing. Observe. Enjoy the scenery. Smooth your hair. Stretch your limbs. Look around and smell the air. Rub your body parts where they feel sore from working or playing. Lean back and breathe in with long deep breaths. Exhale with little sounds of relief.

You will be amazed how little it takes to restore yourself with a personal timeout.

Sleep well and rest often. A good nature depends on good sleep.

How many times have you realized that your day would have gone better if you had just gotten more rest? It is easier if you get in rhythm with the sunrise and the sunset, however antiquated that may sound. If you can't get to bed at a decent hour, then take a fine catnap during the day. No decision will be better made by staying up late.

Roll on the ground every now and then, but do not forget where terra firma is.

So many of you are reluctant to get on the ground and roll around. Perhaps it is because you are often trying to get up, get it up, get high, get ahead, and get going. Rolling on the ground may seem meaningless and completely unproductive, but a good roll is unlike any other remedy for balancing out the manic pace of human life.

When you loosen up enough to roll around on the ground and perhaps even giggle, it can instantly transport you to a time when life was fun and playful and maybe even preciously silly.

Drink mostly water, as that is the beverage you need most, and it will keep you clear and youthful and bring a glow to your hair.

People are always taking a break to drink something. Coffee and tea have become big favorites, along with wine and other alcohol.

Whereas variety is the spice of life, water is the eternal spring of youth. Water cleanses everything in your body. It is like taking a shower inward. Keep your water intake high and you will feel more truly refreshed.

All vices are best enjoyed at lengthy intervals. Do not let a vice nip you with constant cravings.

A little herb. A little sip. A little nooky. A little caviar. A good life!

What makes life delightfully delicious is a specially placed vice along the way. Too much of anything makes life dull and overly accented; it becomes saturated instead of sublime.

Never make a great treat a staple meal. Its novelty will be lost and your senses will become sluggish and less attuned. Ritualize the sacred bliss of partaking in something a little extra.

Excessive appetites should not be fed.

Don't be ashamed if your beast gets the best of you. Some of us really crave more than we should, and we just can't seem to stop the cravings.

We don't all have a *stop* button when it comes to regulating substances. This is when you have to rely on your superior conscience, or your "higher self" to intervene and limit or eliminate your intake of certain things.

Regardless of what your addictive demons are suggesting, there is never a real reward for consuming too much of anything. If you need help with this, that's okay. Sometimes a loving friend will help you stay away from the things that possess you. A group of friends who want you to stay on track is the best.

Spit up instead of swallowing bad feelings or food. It is not that hard to let go of ugly things.

A lot people don't like to "throw up" or "throw away" their mistakes or hurts. They like to nuzzle them into a big ball of thoughts and drama. They like to keep stuff in as if to demonstrate how strong and noble they are.

It feels great to *let go* and *move on*. If you taste something rotten, spit it out. There is no obligation to ingest anything that is bad for you.

If you don't like your food, don't eat it.

If some food really doesn't agree with you, you can politely refrain from eating it.

Popeye ate his spinach because it made him strong. Cleopatra ate caviar because it tasted divine. You can eat things because they are good for you or because they taste great. But if a food is neither important for your health nor something you keenly desire, give it a resounding pass!

Eat more greens when you feel constipated.

There are so many bottles in the medicine cabinet for gas, indigestion, headaches, and constipation. When you start to feel even a little wonky, it is best to eat as many greens as you can. Fresh wheatgrass is best, but if you cannot manage that then a whole plate of leafy greens will work wonders to clean out the other foods that are clogging you up.

The best thing to do to prevent rushing off to buy man-made pills is to make sure that you eat what nature offers in the green variety on a regular basis. Animals have always known to eat green when their digestion feels icky red.

Do not go to the doctor's office for every little thing, if you can help it. Stay fit, be grateful, and focus on what feels good.

Too many of you go to the medicine cabinet instead of living sensibly. If you actually paid attention to the signals your bodies gave you, would be in better shape, eat healthier food, and get more rest. The body is wisely designed to run on simple fuels, rejuvenate with rest, and stay strong through consistent exercise and nonrepetitive movement.

When it is time to die, do not resist. Find a peaceful place and allow your body to rest. Your spirit is free and will continue to love on and on.

People make an awful lot of fuss over dying—as if it wasn't meant to happen. They do extreme things to prevent people from letting go of their earthly bodies. It is much wiser to relish the perfection of the cycles of death and birth, and to seize each moment to celebrate life fully as it is.

MORE FROM STANLEY AND FRIENDS

If you meet the Buddha on the road pet him!

Sometimes all you really need is a little space.

Sharing is Love- even if sometimes it is a little inconvenient.

When making a choice it's best to take your time instead of rushing.

A different view can help gain calm and perspective.

"When you are not ready for someone to leave - put your foot down gently."

Bixby

Stay Connected to Stanley

Go to @stanleythecat on Twitter and Lessons from Stanley the Cat on facebook, and let us know what your beloved animals have taught you?!

Acknowledgments

I would like to thank Tone Gellerstedt for her superb art and understanding of Stanley's sensibility and humor.

My friends MaryAnne Contreras and Marianne Partridge Poett encouraged me in every way. Hilary Dole Klein gave me the key, and the verve, to proceed. Finally I would like to bow to my partner Rendy, who is the blessing of my life and has been gracious, and mostly good-natured, about sharing me with my beloved Stanley.

Please stay in touch with Jennifer at
www.jenniferfreed.com

Artist Tone Gellerstedt and Author Jennifer Freed in Venezuela 2006 - where they met at a Spanish Language intensive.

Printed in Great Britain
by Amazon